The Warrior Mom's Guide to Generational Wealth & Family Legacy

Building Wealth, Purpose, and a Future That Lasts

Author Shaundra M. G. Harris

i

The Warrior Mom's Guide to Generational Wealth & Family Legacy

Building Wealth, Purpose, and a Future That Lasts

Author Shaundra M. G. Harris

Shaun The Mom Publishing

Paperback ISBN : 978-1-969446-02-3

Hardcover SBN: 978-1-969446-12-2

Shaun The Mom Publishing

Printed in the United States.

www.warriormomacademy.com

Disclaimer

This book is intended for informational and inspirational purposes only. The content reflects the personal experiences, opinions, and insights of the author and should not be considered a substitute for professional medical, legal, financial, educational, therapeutic, or spiritual advice.

While the author shares tools, tips, and resources that have been personally helpful, every situation is unique. Readers are encouraged to consult with qualified professionals before making decisions regarding health, finances, homeschooling, parenting, estate planning, or other matters discussed in this book.

Some links or references provided may be affiliate links. This means the author may receive a small commission at no extra cost to you if you choose to purchase through those links. These recommendations are made in good faith and only include resources the author personally uses or believes may be helpful.

Any printable templates, checklists, or workbook materials included are for personal use only and may not be distributed, sold, or used commercially without written permission from the author.

The author and publisher expressly disclaim any liability arising directly or indirectly from the use or misuse of any information, tools, or resources included in this book.

For every mama who dared to dream beyond survival.

To my four beautiful children — Aoki, Layla, Jayden, and Nia

You are the reason I fight, the reason I rise, and the reason I believe in something greater than today.

This book, this business, this mission — it's all for you.

"A good person leaves an inheritance for their children's children."

— Proverbs 13:22 (NIV)

Welcome from the Author

Dear Warrior Mom,

Welcome to your legacy-building space.

To my fellow mothers living with chronic illness —

Your strength is unmatched. Your story matters. May this guide remind you that you are not just surviving — you are building something eternal.

To every woman who's ever felt overlooked, unheard, or underestimated —

May these pages give you a path forward, a blueprint for legacy, and the courage to create wealth that heals.

And to the little girl I once was —

You dreamed of more, even in pain. This is the "more" you knew was possible.

With all my love and legacy,

Shaun

"I am my ancestors' wildest dreams. I am my children's greatest inheritance."

— Unknown

Table of Contents

THE WARRIOR MOM GUIDES

Introduction

Welcome Warrior Moms

I started writing this book from a hospital bed, with an IV in my arm and purpose in my heart.

As a mom living with sickle cell disease, I've had to fight for my life and my children's future — in every way that matters.

There were moments I didn't know how we'd make it — physically, emotionally, financially.

But something inside me refused to let struggle be the end of our story. So I turned my pain into pages, my trials into teaching, and my motherhood into a mission.

Shaun the Mom Publishing started with one book. Then it became a movement. And now, it's a legacy.

This guide is my way of passing on what I've learned — not just to my own children, but to yours, too.

It's for the mom who wants her kids to be ready.

The parent who wants to leave more than just love — but land, leadership, and literacy.

Inside, you'll find tools to:

1. Pay your children through your business (the right way)
2. Teach them how to save, budget, invest, and grow wealth
3. Build systems for long-term impact and family ownership

You don't need to be wealthy to build wealth. You just need the vision, the tools, and the willingness to start.

This guide will help you do all three.

Welcome to the ThriveHive

With heart, hustle, and healing,

Shaun

My Story: From Survival to Legacy

I grew up seeing money as something that slipped through your hands as quickly as it came.

I watched people I loved work themselves to the bone, only to have nothing left at the end of the month.

I knew there had to be a different way, but I didn't know where to start.

Motherhood changed that for me. The moment I held my first child, I felt a responsibility that was bigger than my fear.

It wasn't just about paying bills anymore—it was about showing my kids what was possible.

Over time, I began to study, experiment, and learn what it takes to build real assets and opportunities. I made mistakes, tried again, and kept moving.

Along the way, I discovered that purpose-driven wealth is different from chasing status or appearances.

It's about using every lesson—every hardship—to create something lasting.

If you're reading this, you're probably carrying your own story of struggle and survival.

Maybe you've wondered if it's too late or too hard to leave a meaningful legacy.

I'm here to tell you it's not.

You are exactly where you need to be to start building something extraordinary.

The Power of Purpose-Driven Parenthood

When we parent with purpose, we give our children more than love—we give them a roadmap.

A vision of what's possible.

A way to see themselves as worthy of ownership, stability, and joy.

Purpose-driven parenthood is not about perfection.

It's not about having all the answers or never making mistakes.

It's about showing up with intention—even when it's hard.

When you begin teaching your children about money, ownership, and leadership, you plant seeds that will grow long after you're gone.

Those seeds become the mindset they carry into their own families, businesses, and communities.

This guide exists to help you plant those seeds with confidence.

- Even if no one ever showed you how.
- Even if you're still learning yourself.
- Even if you're starting from scratch.

Part I: Vision & Foundation

Chapter 1: Why This Guide Exists

I wrote this guide in a season when most people would've expected me to give up on big dreams.

It was born in the tension between struggle and strength—through a mother's refusal to let adversity be the final chapter of her story.

I was sitting in a hospital bed with an IV in my arm, wondering how long I'd be there this time.

Sickle cell disease has a way of teaching you about survival in ways you never wanted to learn.

But even on the hardest days, I knew one thing for sure:

Survival couldn't be the end of my story.

I wasn't just fighting for my health—I was fighting for my children to have more than I did:

1. More stability.
2. More ownership.
3. More understanding of how money really works.

I wanted them to know that wealth isn't reserved for the lucky few—it's something that any family can build, even starting with very little.

It's easy to believe that legacy-building starts when you have more time, more money, or more help.

But the truth?

Legacy often begins in the middle of chaos.

It starts while you're still healing.

It starts before you feel ready.

How This Guide Can Transform Your Family's Future

You hold in your hands the blueprint I wish I had when I started.

Inside, you'll find step-by-step guidance to:

1. Legally hire your children and pay them in ways that build their financial literacy
2. Open accounts and create systems that give them a head start
3. Grow your business into a lasting source of wealth
4. Prepare a succession plan so your work lives on

Each chapter will walk you through the process—one clear step at a time.

- You don't need to do everything all at once.
- You don't need to be wealthy already.
- You just need to be willing to begin.

If you're reading this and thinking, "I'm not ready," remember: Legacy is built by ordinary people doing intentional things.

You are exactly the kind of person who can create a future your children will thank you for.

🪴 Reflection | Prayer | Affirmation | Action

Why This Guide Exists

Reflection

1. Take a moment to pause. Grab a journal or open a blank document and explore these:
2. What does "generational wealth" mean to you personally?
3. How has your life experience shaped your beliefs about money and ownership?
4. What are three words you hope your children will use to describe your legacy?
5. What is one fear that has held you back from building wealth?
6. What is one hope that keeps you moving forward?

Affirmation

I am the seed-planter of legacy, not in spite of my struggle—but because of it.

Every small, intentional step I take today creates a foundation my children will stand on tomorrow.

I am worthy of building wealth, and my story is powerful enough to change generations.

Prayer

God, I thank You for the strength to dream, even in the middle of hard seasons.

Help me to see my value beyond my current circumstances.

Remind me that I don't have to be perfect to leave a legacy—just willing, faithful, and intentional.

Guide me as I lay the foundation for something greater than myself.

Bless the work of my hands and let my children rise from the seeds I plant in love. Amen.

Action

Small steps build momentum. This week, commit to these simple actions:

- Write Your Legacy Letter:
  - Draft a one-page letter to your children—or your future self— explaining why you're choosing to build generational wealth.
- Create a Vision Board:
  - Gather images, words, or symbols that represent the legacy you want to build. Place it somewhere you'll see every day.

- Identify Your Values:

  List three core values you want your family's financial future to reflect.

  (Examples: stability, generosity, education.)

You've already taken your first step by reading this chapter.

Keep going—your story is just beginning.

Chapter 2: The Family Business Blueprint

Your family is your first business, and your values are your brand.

Everything you do—from how you communicate to how you budget—is shaping the culture and mission of your family unit.

In this chapter, we'll define how to align your business mission with your family's purpose.

You'll learn how to build a brand that reflects your story and how to involve your children—not just as helpers or employees—but as legacy builders.

When your children understand the "why" behind the work, they rise into their own leadership.

They see the family business not as "mama's hustle," but as a shared inheritance.

That changes everything.

About Shaun the Mom : Building with Purpose

I didn't start a business just to make money.

I started it to change the story my children inherited.

As a single mom living with chronic illness, entrepreneurship became a survival tool—and then a vehicle for empowerment. It allowed me to create income around my health, work with my children beside me, and teach them in real time what ownership looks like.

I wanted my children to know that their last name could mean something. That they didn't have to grow up disconnected from wealth-building just because we started with less.

Family businesses are more than LLCs and logos. They are legacy labs. And you don't need to be a millionaire to start one—you just need to get clear on your values and take consistent steps to build.

Combining Entrepreneurship with Empowerment

The beauty of running a business as a parent is that it becomes a classroom. Every client call, every invoice, every setback becomes a teachable moment.

When children witness your work ethic, your creativity, and even your recovery from failure, they internalize lessons that will outlast any job or paycheck. But when we invite them in—to learn, participate, and contribute—their confidence and identity begin to shift.

You're not just giving them income—you're giving them insight.

And insight turns into ownership.

Defining Your Family's Mission & Values

Your business doesn't need to be fancy or traditional. But it does need to be rooted in something real.

Start by asking:

1. What do we stand for as a family?
2. What are the values we want to be known for?
3. How does our business reflect our personal story?

Whether your business is a cleaning service, an online shop, a homeschool co-op, or a nonprofit—you can define a mission that reflects your roots and your vision for the future.

Here are a few example mission statements:

- We exist to serve single-parent families through affordable tutoring and education.
- Our family brand uplifts the community through handmade products and cultural storytelling.
- We teach financial literacy to youth in our neighborhood because wealth starts with knowledge.

You don't have to get it perfect—you just have to get it personal.

🐝 Reflection | Prayer | Affirmation | Action

The Family Business Blueprint

Reflection

Take a quiet moment to reflect or journal:

1. What does your family stand for?
2. What do you want your children to learn from watching you work?
3. How does your current business (or business idea) align with your values?
4. What are some creative ways your children could participate?
5. How would your business look different if it were built for legacy—not just income?

Affirmation

I am not just building a business.

I am building a legacy rooted in love, values, and vision.

My family is my first enterprise, and we rise together.

Prayer

God, Thank You for planting the seed of vision in my heart.

Help me build something that honors You and nourishes my family.

Give me the wisdom to align our business with our values,

The courage to invite my children into the journey,

And the patience to grow step by step, season by season.

Let our work be more than hustle—let it be holy. Amen.

Action

Start where you are. One step at a time.

- Write a Family Mission Statement
  - What does your family business stand for? Draft 2–3 lines that define your purpose and values.
- Create a Family Values List
  - Have each family member choose one value that matters to them. Combine

the answers into your official "family business values."

- Make a Legacy Plan Together
  - Ask your children what kind of impact they want to make. Dream together. Create a "Legacy Vision Board" with words or pictures.
- Name the Business Together (if you haven't yet)
  - Choose a name that reflects your family's purpose and pride. Let your kids be part of the naming and branding process.

Part II: Legally Hiring Your Children

Chapter 3: Creating Real Jobs for Your Kids

One of the most powerful decisions you can make as a parent is to treat your children as capable contributors—not passive observers.

When you give your kids real, meaningful work in your business, you do more than teach them skills. You teach them to believe they belong in spaces of ownership.

You show them that wealth is not handed down by chance—it is built, step by step, through intention and action.

In this chapter, you'll learn how to identify age-appropriate roles, create clear expectations, and begin compensating your children for their contributions.

Whether your business is online, in-person, or a mix of both, there is always a place for your children to grow alongside you.

Why Early Work Matters

Many of us grew up thinking that "real work" started after high school or college. But the truth is, children can learn responsibility, problem-solving, and the value of their time much earlier than that—especially when we give them the chance.

Involving them in your business allows you to:

1. Build confidence. They see their ideas and effort make a real difference.
2. Teach discipline. They learn how to show up, follow through, and take initiative.
3. Foster ownership. They begin to feel invested in your family's shared success.
4. Develop skills. From customer service to tech tools, these early experiences compound over time.

Let's be clear—this isn't about using your kids for free labor. It's about honoring their gifts and giving them a foundation of self-worth, work ethic, and wealth literacy.

Age-Appropriate Job Titles & Duties

Every child is different, but here are practical examples of real roles children can fill—based on age and ability.

Example: A Family Book Business

Age 10 (Junior Assistant)

- Organize printed drafts and supplies
- Pack and label book orders
- Sort or count inventory for events

Age 12 (Content Helper)

- Create simple graphics using templates (like Canva)
- Proofread short materials with help
- Track inventory or sales on a chart or checklist

Age 15 (Marketing Assistant)

- Draft social media captions
- Help design flyers or promo materials
- Update mailing lists or manage giveaways

Age 20 (Project Coordinator)

- Manage production and launch timelines
- Oversee fulfillment systems
- Coordinate email newsletters and outreach

Example: A YouTube Channel

Age 10

- Set up lighting or props
- Help organize recording space
- Brainstorm video ideas

Age 12

- Edit short clips (with guidance)
- Create thumbnails using Canva
- Moderate comments under supervision

Age 15

- Schedule uploads and manage playlists
- Research keywords or video topics
- Monitor basic analytics

Age 20

- Plan monthly content calendars
- Negotiate with sponsors
- Analyze data and optimize performance

Example: A Vending Machine Business

Age 10

- Help stock snacks and drinks
- Clean machine surfaces
- Count and roll coins

Age 12

- Record inventory levels
- Assist with reordering supplies
- Create labels or price signage

Age 15

- Track sales trends
- Update Google Sheets or Excel logs
- Design marketing flyers or social posts

Age 20

- Manage vendor or supplier relationships
- Handle scheduling and repairs
- Oversee deposits and bookkeeping

Tip: Write a clear, simple job description for each child. Post it somewhere visible. This sets expectations and builds confidence.

Teaching Professionalism Through Purpose

It's important to treat these roles as real jobs—not just "helping out" or doing chores. That starts with mindset and language.

When you pay your children for their work, you reinforce powerful truths:

- Their time has value.
- Their contributions matter.
- Work done with purpose is rewarding.

Ways to Reinforce Professionalism:

- Set a schedule. Even 2–3 hours a week builds consistency.
- Offer training. Show them how to complete tasks step by step.
- Give feedback. Praise what's going well and coach through challenges.
- Pay fairly. Compensation should reflect age, ability, and legal compliance (more on that in Chapter 4).

You are not just training workers. You are nurturing confident, capable builders of legacy.

🦋 Reflection | Prayer | Affirmation | Action

Creating Real Jobs for Your Kids

Reflection

Take a quiet moment to think or journal:

1. What early work experiences shaped you as a child or teen?
2. How could involving your children help them feel more confident and capable?
3. Which of your children's strengths would thrive in a business role?
4. What boundaries or expectations do you want to set in advance?
5. How will you celebrate their contributions as they grow?

Affirmation

My children are not just helpers—they are co-builders of a legacy.

I am equipping them with confidence, skills, and vision.

Together, we are planting seeds of wealth, wisdom, and purpose.

Prayer

Dear Lord, Thank You for the gift of my children and the dreams You've placed in our hearts. Help me see their potential and trust them with real responsibility.

Teach me how to guide them with grace and structure, how to affirm their efforts, and how to lead by example.

May our family business become a garden of growth, where they learn to work with joy, purpose, and integrity. Amen.

Action

Choose at least two of these to complete this week:

- Draft Job Descriptions
    - Use the examples in this chapter and write out duties for each child.
- Schedule a Work Orientation
    - Block out time to teach them how to do their role step-by-step.
- Create a Work Log
    - Use a notebook, form, or spreadsheet to track hours and tasks.
- Pick a Start Date
    - Mark it on the calendar and treat it like a launch day.

- Discuss Pay
  - Talk about wages and explain how and when they'll get paid (we'll handle legal/payroll in Chapter 4).

When your children see themselves as valued team members, they learn a truth many adults still struggle to believe:

They are worthy of purpose, contribution, and compensation.

Chapter 4: Legal Payroll — How to Pay Your Children the Right Way

Paying your children through your family business isn't just about handing over money is a transformative act — one that teaches them the value of work, responsibility, and financial stewardship.

It breaks cycles of silence around money and equips your family with tools for generational wealth.

When you pay your children the right way, you're not just cutting a check—you're cutting through generations of fear, limitation, and lack.

You're modeling a new truth: that their time matters, their gifts matter, and there's power in purpose-driven pay.

But to do it right, you need to follow legal payroll rules to protect your business and your family.

Setting Fair Wage Rates

Wages should match the task, your child's age, and their skill level. The goal is fairness and consistency, not perfection.

Example wage ranges:

- A 10-year-old packing book orders might earn $8/hour.
- A 15-year-old writing YouTube captions could earn $11/hour.
- A 20-year-old managing marketing calendars might earn $18/hour.

Step 1: Create and Use Timesheets

Tracking hours worked is essential for legal compliance and payroll accuracy.

Each child should keep a timesheet that includes:

- Date worked
- Hours worked
- Specific tasks performed
- Parent or supervisor signature to verify the work

Timesheets can be paper forms or simple digital spreadsheets. The important part is that they are consistently completed and stored.

Step 2: Run Payroll Correctly

You have options for paying your children:

- Payroll Software: Tools like Gusto or QuickBooks Payroll make tax withholding, pay stubs, and filing easier.
- Manual Payroll: Use spreadsheets to calculate hours and pay, then pay by check or bank transfer.
- Tax Withholding: Depending on your business structure (sole proprietorship, corporation, etc.), you may or may not need to withhold Social Security, Medicare, or income taxes for your children. Check IRS guidelines or consult a tax professional.

Step 3: Issue Year-End Tax Forms

Even though it's family, you still need to treat payments like any employee:

- Issue a W-2 form to your child by January 31 each year. This reports their income to the IRS and helps them file their taxes properly.
- Keep copies of these forms for your records.

Step 4: Keep Detailed Records

Maintain organized files for at least four years containing:

- Job descriptions

- Signed work agreements
- Timesheets
- Pay records
- Tax filings

Good records protect your family business during IRS audits and ensure everyone stays compliant.

Why This Matters: Tax Benefits and Smart Strategies

Now here's where things get exciting.

Paying your children through your business can save money and build wealth—if done correctly.

Deductible Wages:

- You can deduct wages paid to your children as a legitimate business expense, reducing your taxable income.

Standard Deduction for Kids:

- Children can earn up to $13,850 tax-free (2023 limit, update yearly). This means their earned income might not be taxed, allowing you to legally shift income within your family.

Roth IRAs for Kids:

- With earned income, you can open a Roth IRA for your child. This tax-advantaged account grows their money tax-free over decades—setting them up for a secure financial future.

Teaching Financial Responsibility Through Payroll

Money is not just payment—it's a powerful lesson.

When your children are paid through the business, they learn:

- Their time and work have value.
- Work requires accountability and documentation.
- Managing income responsibly starts early.

Encourage your children to split their earnings into three "buckets":

- Saving (for emergencies and future goals)
- Spending (for personal use and freedom)
- Giving (for tithes and charitable causes)

This simple practice builds lifelong money habits.

🐝 Reflection | Prayer | Affirmation | Action

Legal Payroll — How to Pay Your Children the Right Way

Reflection Questions

1. What feelings do you have about paying your children a wage?
2. How can a paycheck help your child develop confidence and financial independence?
3. What systems will help you stay compliant and organized?
4. What lessons about work and money do you want your child to learn through this process?
5. Who can you consult for help with payroll and taxes?

Affirmation

"I honor my children's contributions by compensating them fairly and legally. Together, we build a legacy of work ethic, responsibility, and financial wisdom."

Prayer

Dear God,

Thank You for the gift of family and the opportunity to teach my children through work and stewardship.

Grant me wisdom to manage our business with integrity and fairness.

May every paycheck remind my children of their worth and their purpose.

Guide us to build a legacy that honors You and empowers future generations. Amen.

Action

Choose two to begin this week:

- Select a payroll method (software or manual) that fits your business.
- Create a timesheet template that records essential details.
- Set fair and consistent wage rates for each child based on their role.
- Hold a family meeting to explain the payroll process, including taxes and responsibilities.
- Schedule a consultation with a tax professional to ensure you're following the law.

Part III: Financial Systems for Now & Later

Chapter 5: Smart Money Tools for Every Age

Once you've begun paying your children for their contributions, the next step is helping them manage and grow their earnings.

This is where most families stop short. They hand over paychecks but never show their kids how to make money work for them.

In this chapter, we'll walk through the essential financial tools you can set up for your children—no matter their age. These tools will empower them to:

1. Save for goals they care about
2. Build credit responsibly
3. Invest early and watch their money grow
4. Develop lifelong confidence in handling finances

The best part? You don't have to be wealthy to start. Every account can be opened with small amounts— and big dreams.

Why Start Early?

Most people don't learn about compound interest, credit scores, or investment basics until adulthood— when mistakes can cost thousands of dollars.

But imagine this:

- Your 10-year-old has a savings account where they watch their earnings grow.
- Your 15-year-old has a Roth IRA that could be worth six figures by the time they retire.
- Your 20-year-old already has a positive credit history and understands how to budget.

This isn't fantasy. This is the power of starting early and making financial literacy part of your family culture.

Checking & Savings Accounts

Ages 8–13: Youth Savings Accounts

1. Great for learning the basics of deposits, withdrawals, and goal-setting
2. Many banks offer no-fee accounts for minors

Examples:

- Capital One Kids Savings Account
- Alliant Credit Union Kids Savings
- Chase first checking

Ages 13–17: Teen Checking Accounts

1. Helps teens practice with debit cards and basic budgeting
2. Allows parents to monitor spending with alerts and restrictions

Examples:

- Capital One MONEY Teen Checking
- Chase High School Checking

Teaching Tip:

When you set these up, walk your child through:

- How to read a bank statement
- How to check balances
- How to create and track savings goals

Roth IRAs & Investing Early

This is one of the biggest wealth hacks for kids. Any child with earned income can open a Roth IRA.

- Contributions are made after-tax
- Growth is tax-free forever
- Contributions can be withdrawn anytime (earnings should stay invested)

Example:

If your 15-year-old contributes $2,000 per year from ages 15 to 20, and the money grows at 7% annually, it could be worth $120,000+ by age 60.

Where to open:

- Fidelity Youth Roth IRA (ages 13–17)
- Vanguard Roth IRA (custodial)

How to fund:

They can contribute up to the amount they earned (within the IRS annual limit).

Custodial Brokerage Accounts & 529 Plans

Custodial Brokerage Account (UGMA/UTMA):

1. Invest in stocks, ETFs, or mutual funds
2. Transfers to your child at age 18–21
3. Can be used for non-education expenses

529 College Savings Plan:

1. Tax-free growth for qualified education expenses
2. Many states offer tax deductions or credits for contributions

How to Choose: Use a 529 for college.

Use a Custodial Brokerage Account for broader goals like a first home or starting a business.

Credit Building for Teens & Young Adults

Teaching your older kids to build credit responsibly can save them from costly mistakes later.

Ages 18+:

1. Add them as an authorized user on your credit card
2. Help them get a secured credit card with a small deposit

Credit Success Tips:

- Always pay balances in full
- Keep credit utilization under 30%
- Never co-sign for something you can't afford

Your Family Example in Action

Here's how you might implement these tools by age:

🐾 Age 10:

- Youth Savings Account
- Weekly deposits from vending machine work

🐾 Age 12:

- Teen Checking Account
- Custodial Brokerage with small monthly investments

🌿 Age 15:

- Teen Checking Account
- Roth IRA funded by YouTube or small business work

🌿 Age 20:

- Credit card for credit building
- Roth IRA + 529 Plan for education or future goals

When you introduce these tools gradually, you're giving your children power over their financial future—not just for today, but for generations to come.

🦋 Reflection | Prayer | Affirmation | Action

Smart Money Tools for Every Age

Reflection Questions

Pause and consider:

1. What financial lessons do you wish you had learned as a child?
2. How do you feel about teaching your children to invest or save?
3. What fears or concerns come up when you think about money?
4. What's one financial milestone you want to celebrate with your child this year?

Affirmation

"I am equipping my children with tools to break cycles and build generational wealth. We are creating a legacy rooted in wisdom, not fear."

Family Prayer

Dear God,

Thank You for providing not just enough, but opportunities to grow beyond survival.

Help me guide my children in managing money with wisdom, integrity, and grace.

Teach us together how to steward every blessing with purpose, and may every seed we plant financially yield peace and prosperity for generations. Amen.

Action

Choose at least two to complete this week:

- Open a Starter Account. A youth savings or checking account is a simple but powerful first step.
- Set a Shared Savings Goal. Even $50 saved toward a goal helps develop financial motivation.
- Host a "Money Talk." Explain interest, budgets, or Roth IRAs using real examples your child understands.
- Create a Visual Tracker. A printed thermometer or goal chart makes progress feel real.
- Research Roth IRAs. If your child has earned income, look into opening an account to start building wealth now.

Every financial tool you introduce is a gift. With each step, you're not just teaching money skills— you're planting legacy.

Chapter 6: Budgeting, Saving & Spending as a Family

Money doesn't have to be a secret.

Money doesn't have to be a stressor.

In fact, when you talk openly about how money flows in and out of your family, you transform finances from something mysterious into something empowering.

This chapter is about turning everyday moments—like grocery shopping, paying bills, or planning a family outing—into lifelong lessons. When you budget, save, and spend as a family, you teach your children to:

1. Make thoughtful choices
2. Delay gratification
3. Align money with values

Even small practices, done consistently, shape how your children see themselves and what they believe is possible.

Why Family Budgeting Matters

Children learn by watching.

If they never see you set a budget, they won't know budgeting is normal.

If they never hear you talk about saving, they'll assume spending it all is what grown-ups do.

If they never experience giving, they'll believe money is only for themselves.

When you invite your children into money conversations—at any age—you give them a gift many of us never received: financial literacy rooted in love, not fear.

Creating a Family Budget

A budget is simply a plan for how you want to use your money.

Here's a kid-friendly formula to introduce:

Income – Giving – Saving – Expenses = What's Left to Spend

Break your family budget into three simple buckets:

- ◆ Needs: Rent, food, utilities, healthcare
- ◆ Goals: Debt payoff, savings, big purchases
- ◆ Joy: Fun money, outings, extras

When planning your monthly budget, include:

1. Household expenses
2. Business expenses
3. Children's wages and savings
4. Giving (tithes, donations, helping family)

Tool Tip: Use an app like YNAB, EveryDollar, or Goodbudget, or keep it simple with a printable worksheet taped to the fridge.

Setting Savings Goals as a Family

Saving becomes powerful when it's personal.

Choose:

- One shared family goal (e.g. saving $1,500 for a trip)
- One personal goal per child (e.g. a bike, gaming system, or college fund)

When your child sees their hard work—like stocking a vending machine or filming a video—help the whole family reach a goal, they feel proud and empowered.

Spending with Intention

Spending is part of life.

But spending without awareness is how even high-earning families go broke.

Teach your children to pause and ask:

- Do I truly want this, or is it just an impulse?
- Is this aligned with my goals and values?
- Will this choice delay or derail my savings?

Use the 48-Hour Rule:

If you want something big, wait two days.

If you still want it and it fits the budget, go for it.

If not, let it go.

Age-Appropriate Budgeting Conversations

Here's how to tailor budgeting talks to different ages:

- Age 10

"We earned $200 this week. Let's save $20, give $10, and use the rest for groceries and fun."

"Let's compare prices while we shop together."

- Age 12

"How much do you want to save from your vending machine pay this month?"

"Can you track how much we spend on groceries this week?"

- Age 15

"Let's compare phone plans together."

"Want to create a personal budget for your earnings?"

- Age 20

"This is how I track bills and savings. Want help creating your own system?"

"Let's make a budget for living on your own."

Tools & Apps to Make It Fun

Greenlight Debit Card: Kids track spending, set goals, and learn budgeting

GoHenry: Prepaid debit card designed for younger kids

YNAB: Great for older teens and young adults learning zero-based budgeting

Printable Trackers: Use charts or color-in savings thermometers for little ones

🦋 Reflection | Prayer | Affirmation | Action

Budgeting, Saving & Spending as a Family

Reflection Questions

Pause and consider:

1. What budgeting habits do I want my children to learn from me?
2. How transparent am I willing to be about money?
3. What's one small change I can make to bring consistency to our budget?
4. What money wounds or fears am I still carrying?
5. How can I make budgeting feel joyful instead of heavy?

Affirmation

I am creating a legacy of wisdom, not worry.

Money flows in my family with purpose, peace, and power.

Together, we are learning, growing, and building a future rooted in faith and freedom.

Prayer

Dear God, Thank You for being my provider, my peace, and my source of wisdom.

Help me to lead my family with grace as we learn to steward money with purpose.

Give me courage to break unhealthy patterns, and the clarity to teach my children financial truth—rooted in love, not fear.

Bless our efforts, Lord. Let every lesson, every budget, and every sacrifice become a seed of generational growth.

May we use our resources not just for survival, but to build a life of joy, generosity, and purpose. Amen.

Action

Choose at least two this week:

- Schedule a Family Budget Night. Set a date to sit down and plan the month together.
- Define a Shared Goal. Choose something everyone can save toward.
- Create a Visual Tracker. Use a chart your kids can color in or update weekly.
- Pick One Tool or App. Set it up and walk your child through it.

- Practice the 48-Hour Rule. Talk through at least one buying decision together.

When you budget, save, and spend with intention, you're not just teaching financial skills—you're modeling ownership, wisdom, and freedom.

You're giving your children a head start on a life where money serves their dreams, not controls them.

Chapter 7: Using Your Business to Build Wealth

You didn't start your business just to pay the bills.

You started it because you wanted to create something bigger—a legacy that could outlast you.

Your business is more than a source of income.

It's a vehicle for generational wealth, family ownership, and lasting impact.

This chapter will help you look beyond the day-to-day hustle and think strategically about building long-term revenue streams, reinvesting in your children's future, and positioning your business as a valuable asset for decades to come.

The Power of Small Businesses

Some people think wealth only comes from corporate jobs or inheritance.

But here's the truth:

Small business is one of the most powerful and accessible tools for financial freedom—especially for moms like us.

- You control the vision and direction.
- You can legally hire and train your children.
- You build intellectual property, systems, and skills that grow over time.
- You create trust, community, and credibility that compound in value.

Whether you run a vending machine route, a YouTube channel, a publishing imprint, or something else entirely—your business can and should be built to multiply your mission and income.

Expanding Your Income Streams

One of the biggest mistakes small business owners make is relying on just one stream of income.

Multiple income streams = more security, more opportunity, and more options.

They protect you when life throws curveballs and help your business grow faster.

Here are some streams you might consider:

Books & Digital Products

- Write and self-publish guides (like this one!)
- Create downloadable planners, templates, or workbooks
- Offer low-cost eBooks or digital mini-courses

YouTube & Online Content

- Monetize your channel with ads
- Offer exclusive content via Patreon or paid memberships
- Partner with brands for sponsorships

Speaking & Teaching

- Host workshops for moms, youth, or new entrepreneurs
- Offer 1:1 coaching or group sessions
- Speak at schools or local organizations

Physical Products

- Sell merchandise (journals, apparel, tote bags)
- Bundle products with books or courses

Vending Machine Business

- Expand into new locations
- Negotiate contracts with local businesses
- Use vending profits to fund other ventures

Tip: Start with one or two new streams that feel manageable. Build slowly and sustainably.

Reinvesting in Your Children's Future

Instead of pulling every dollar out of your business for survival, choose to set aside a portion to build for the future:

- Fund Roth IRAs for your children
- Save for college, vocational training, or special needs care
- Invest in equipment to scale your business
- Pay your children to build their skills and ownership mindset

Example:

If your YouTube channel earns $2,000/month:

- 40% = Household expenses
- 20% = Business reinvestment
- 20% = Taxes
- 10% = Savings/investments
- 10% = Children's pay

These small choices stack over time—and lead to generational change.

Using Grants and Funding Opportunities

Grants are one of the most underused resources among small business owners—especially women of color.

There are grants specifically for:

- Women-owned businesses
- Minority-owned businesses
- Disability-owned businesses
- Entrepreneurs in underserved communities

Examples:

- Amber Grant for Women
- FedEx Small Business Grant
- Local Chamber of Commerce programs

Action Tip: Set aside one hour per month to apply for grants. Even one approval could fund equipment, hiring, or marketing for your next big step.

Documenting and Protecting Your Assets

Your business isn't just products and services. The real value is in:

- Your brand (name, reputation, logo)
- Your content (videos, courses, books)
- Your systems (emails, customer lists, SOPs)

Protect your legacy:

1. Trademark your brand when possible
2. Keep clean financial records
3. Create Standard Operating Procedures (SOPs)

4. Backup your digital content in multiple places

These steps help ensure your business can outlive you—and continue to bless your family.

Family Involvement & Ownership

Children who see themselves as part of your business develop pride, responsibility, and entrepreneurial confidence.

Ways to build ownership:

- Share monthly profit/loss reports (kid-friendly)
- Ask for their ideas, solutions, or product feedback
- Set revenue goals together
- Celebrate every win as a team

Over time, this becomes more than "mom's business."

It becomes our family legacy.

🐝 Reflection | Prayer | Affirmation | Action

Using Your Business to Build Wealth

Reflection

1. What income streams feel most aligned with your vision?
2. How much are you currently reinvesting into your business?
3. Do your children know your business goals or why you started it?
4. What systems or content need to be documented?
5. What would it mean for your children to co-own this business one day?

Affirmation

My business is a seed planted with love, watered with wisdom, and rooted in legacy.

I am building more than income—I am building freedom for my family, and purpose for generations to come.

Prayer

Dear God,

Thank You for giving me the vision to build something meaningful.

Guide me as I grow this business—not just for survival, but for legacy.

Help me steward every resource with wisdom and generosity.

Give me the courage to dream bigger, the strategy to multiply, and the discipline to teach my children through example.

May this business become a blessing far beyond what I can see today. Amen.

Action

Choose at least two this week:

- Map Your Income Streams – List all current and potential ones
- Pick One New Stream – Outline your next 3 action steps
- Set a Reinvestment Plan – Define a percentage to set aside monthly
- Research One Grant – Spend 30 minutes this week applying
- Draft One SOP – Pick a process (like packing orders or posting videos) and write it down

Chapter 8: The Ownership & Succession Plan

What will happen to your business, your mission, and your impact when you're no longer here to run it?

This is a question many entrepreneurs avoid because it feels overwhelming—or too far in the future to matter.

But here's the truth:

If you don't create a plan, someone else will.

Succession planning isn't just about preparing for the end of life.

It's about:

1. Creating security for your children.
2. Building a bridge for them to step into leadership confidently.
3. Protecting what you worked so hard to build.

This chapter will guide you step-by-step in creating an ownership and succession plan—so your business can thrive for generations.

Why Succession Planning Matters

Without a clear plan:

- Your business could be sold, closed, or contested.
- Your children may not know how to manage or access assets.
- The wealth you've created could be diminished by taxes or legal fees.

When you plan ahead, you ensure that:

1. Your family knows your wishes.
2. Your systems are organized and accessible.
3. Ownership transitions smoothly—whether gradually or after an emergency.

Defining What You're Passing Down

Your business is more than inventory or bank accounts.

It includes:

1. Brand Assets: Your name, logo, website, content.
2. Intellectual Property: Books, videos, courses, proprietary processes.
3. Customer Lists and Contracts: Your relationships and agreements.

4. Physical Assets: Equipment, vending machines, office supplies.
5. Business Accounts: PayPal, Stripe, banking, royalties.
6. Online Presence: YouTube channels, social media, email lists.

Action Tip: Make a master list of all assets so nothing gets overlooked.

Options for Transferring Ownership

Depending on your situation, you have several options:

1. Gradual Transfer:

Your children begin co-managing while you're still active, handing over decision-making step by step.

2. Full Transfer on a Timeline:

You pick a retirement date and sign over ownership fully at that time.

3. Succession After Death or Disability:

Your estate plan specifies who inherits the business and how it will be run or liquidated.

Many families combine these approaches—growing involvement gradually while preparing for emergencies.

Preparing Your Children for Ownership

Naming your children as successors isn't enough—you must prepare them to succeed.

Ways to do this:

- Involve Them Early: Let them shadow you during key decisions. Have them help with finances, marketing, and operations.
- Teach Systems and Processes: Document standard operating procedures (SOPs). Walk them through software, passwords, and key contacts.
- Model Leadership: Share your decision-making process. Explain not just what you do—but why you do it.
- Create Leadership Roles: Give each child age-appropriate responsibilities to build confidence and skills.

Protecting Your Brand and Future

If you want your business to stay in the family, take these protective steps:

1. Formal Operating Agreements: Specify ownership shares, voting rights, buyout options, and decision-making authority.
2. Trademarks and Copyrights: Secure legal protection for your name, logo, and proprietary content.

3. Business Insurance: Consider key person insurance to help cover costs if something happens to you.
4. Estate Plan and Will: Include your business in your estate documents with clear instructions for inheritance.
5. Digital Asset Plan: Store passwords and account details securely, with a trusted person designated to access them if needed.

How This Looks for Your Family

Here's an example of how children's involvement can grow over time:

Age 10: Shadow you while stocking vending machines. Help pack book orders and learn inventory basics.

Age 12: Assist with YouTube video descriptions and analytics. Begin learning bookkeeping basics.

Age 15: Take on more responsibility for marketing and outreach. Learn to use publishing software.

Age 20: Help manage payroll, contracts, and customer relationships. Prepare to co-own the business.

This gradual approach builds their confidence and competence over time.

🐝 Reflection | Prayer | Affirmation | Action

The Ownership & Succession Plan

Reflection Questions

1. What would you want your children to do with your business if you were no longer here?
2. Which child (or children) are most interested in leading or inheriting?
3. What knowledge or skills do they still need to feel ready?
4. How would it feel to know everything is organized and protected?
5. Who can help you create or review these plans (attorney, accountant, advisor)?

Affirmation

I am a wise steward of my business legacy.

I prepare with intention, clarity, and love so my family can carry our mission forward with confidence and purpose.

Prayer

Dear God,

Thank You for the vision and strength to build a business rooted in purpose.

Help me plan wisely and lovingly for the future.

Guide my children as they learn to lead with integrity and courage.

Grant us peace knowing that what we build today will bless generations to come. Amen.

Action

Pick at least two to complete this month:

- Make a Master List of Assets—include content, accounts, inventory, contracts.
- Draft an Ownership Transfer Plan—outline how and when you'd hand off responsibilities.
- Document Key Processes—start with one (inventory, publishing, video production).
- Schedule a Family Meeting—talk openly about your wishes and invite questions.
- Meet with an Estate Planning Attorney— ensure your business is included in your will and legally protected.

Part V: Education, Giving & Impact

Chapter 9: Raising Financially Empowered Kids

You don't need to be a financial expert to raise money-smart children.

You just need to be willing to teach what you learn—and live what you teach.

Financial empowerment doesn't happen overnight. It's built one conversation, one choice, one lesson at a time.

In this chapter, we'll explore how to make money a natural, age-appropriate topic in your home—without shame or pressure.

By modeling healthy financial behaviors and inviting your kids into the process, you raise children who:

1. Know how to manage, grow, and give money.
2. Understand their value beyond what they earn.
3. Step into adulthood with tools, not just dreams.

Why Financial Literacy Starts at Home

Most schools don't teach budgeting, credit, or wealth-building.

If children don't learn these lessons at home, they often enter adulthood unprepared—no matter how smart they are.

As a mother—especially one managing chronic illness and possibly running a family business—your everyday life becomes a classroom. Whether it's grocery shopping on a budget, making business decisions, or paying bills, your kids are always watching.

So instead of shielding them from money talk, invite them in—with openness and love.

What Every Child Should Know by 10, 15, and 20

By Age 10:

- Know the difference between needs and wants
- Save for short-term goals (with jars or a savings account)
- Help with basic money exchanges (change, small purchases)

By Age 15:

- Use a debit card responsibly
- Create and stick to a basic budget
- Understand compound interest
- Begin learning about investing (with support)

By Age 20:

- Manage checking/savings accounts
- Know how credit works and how to build it
- File taxes (with support)
- Contribute to a Roth IRA or investment account
- Understand passive income and business growth

This isn't about strict timelines—it's about consistent exposure and real-life learning.

Everyday Opportunities to Teach Money

Teaching money doesn't have to be formal or forced.

Here's how to weave it into your family rhythm:

Business Tasks:

- Calculate profits
- Price products
- Review marketing results

Shopping Trips:

- Compare prices and brands
- Let them manage a small budget
- Talk about quality vs. quantity

Family Planning:

- Involve them in big decisions (vacations, purchases)
- Discuss trade-offs and priorities

Mistakes as Lessons:

- Walk them through overspending or missed savings
- Frame mistakes as learning moments—not failures

Making It Positive and Age-Appropriate

Many adults feel uncomfortable talking about money because of how we were raised—especially if we experienced lack, guilt, or stress.

But this is your chance to rewrite that story.

Make money talk:

- Safe – No shame, just learning
- Frequent – Regular, not rare
- Relational – A shared journey, not a lecture

You're creating generational healing, not just financial knowledge.

Family Conversations That Build Confidence

Try prompts like:

1. "What happens when someone doesn't have a budget?"
2. "If you earned $100, how would you divide it between spending, saving, and giving?"
3. "What would you love to own, create, or fund someday?"
4. "Want to learn how interest can work for you?"

Create a "Wealth Words" Glossary

Make learning fun with a family glossary of money terms like:

- Budget
- Credit
- ROI (Return on Investment)
- Legacy
- Compound Interest
- Passive Income
- Inheritance

Use drawings, flashcards, or short family lessons. It doesn't have to be fancy—just consistent.

🕮 Reflection | Prayer | Affirmation | Action

Raising Financially Empowered Kids

Reflection Questions

1. What's your earliest memory of money—was it positive or stressful?
2. What kind of money legacy do you want to leave your kids?
3. Which child is showing curiosity about money right now?
4. What beliefs about money are you ready to release?

Affirmation

"I am breaking cycles and building legacy. I teach my children how to use money as a tool for freedom, purpose, and impact."

Prayer

Dear Lord, Thank You for giving me wisdom to raise financially empowered children. Help me to lead by example with humility and grace.

Remove any shame or fear tied to my past experiences, and replace them with courage, knowledge, and faith.

Let my children walk in wisdom and overflow with purpose. May they use wealth not only to build their dreams—but to bless others. Amen.

Action

Choose at least two:

- Teach one financial term this week
- Have a light, fun family "money chat"
- Create a savings tracker for a shared goal
- Review an old receipt together
- Give your child a new money-related business task

Chapter 10: Teaching Purpose Through Giving

Wealth isn't just about what you keep—it's about what you give.

Giving is one of the most powerful ways to teach your children:

1. Compassion
2. Responsibility
3. Purpose greater than themselves

When your children see that money can heal, restore, and uplift, they learn that prosperity is not just accumulation—it's about impact.

This chapter will walk you through simple, age-appropriate ways to build a family culture of generosity—where your legacy is defined not just by what you own, but by what you give.

Why Giving Belongs in Your Legacy

Many of us were taught that giving comes after wealth.

But here's the truth:

- Generosity is a mindset, not a tax bracket
- Even small acts of giving teach that abundance multiplies when shared
- Giving teaches joy, mission, and community

When your children understand that business success can bless others, they'll see money as a mission—not just a means.

The Benefits of Family Giving

Giving can help your kids:

- Build empathy and gratitude
- See value beyond materialism
- Strengthen family bonds
- Create lasting memories rooted in service
- Anchor your identity in contribution

Creating Family Giving Rituals

You don't need to wait for wealth or big milestones. Try:

- Giving Jar: Save a portion of profits or allowances together
- Monthly Missions: Pick a new cause to support each month

- Birthday Giving: Donate a portion of birthday/holiday money
- Family Volunteering: Serve together—meals, cleanups, drives
- Business for Good: Set aside a % of profits to give back

Example:

Your child donates 5% of vending profits to fund school supplies. They feel empowered and purposeful—not just generous.

Age-Appropriate Ways to Teach Giving

Age 10:

- Add to the giving jar
- Help choose a cause
- Write a thank-you to someone inspiring

Age 12:

- Research charities
- Volunteer at a local drive
- Share why they care about a cause

Age 15:

- Budget for giving
- Lead a mini fundraiser

- Connect giving to values

Age 20:

- Set personal giving goals
- Learn how nonprofits work
- Plan long-term contributions

Conversations That Inspire Generosity

Try asking:

1. "If you could help any cause, what would it be?"
2. "How does it feel when you give to others?"
3. "What do you want our family to be known for?"
4. "How can we use our business to make a difference?"

Legacy Isn't Just About Money

When you teach your children to give, you show them:

- Money is a tool for good
- Success includes service
- Legacy is defined by impact

Imagine how powerful it will be for your children to grow up knowing they are blessed to be a blessing.

🕮 Reflection | Prayer | Affirmation | Action

Teaching Purpose Through Giving

Reflection Questions

1. What role did giving play in your childhood?
2. What causes stir your heart as a family?
3. What giving memory would you love to create together?
4. How can you show joyful generosity—even with limited resources?

Affirmation

"My family is rooted in compassion. We give joyfully, serve faithfully, and create impact far beyond ourselves."

Prayer

God of abundance, Thank You for trusting me with the opportunity to give.

Help me model joyful generosity to my children—so they grow up knowing that wealth is more than money.

Let our giving be a light that draws others to Your love.

Use even our small acts to create ripples of change.

Make our legacy one of faith, service, and compassion. Amen.

Action

Try at least two:

- Start a Giving Jar
- Pick one cause and research it
- Have a Family Giving Night (watch a doc, then discuss)
- Donate together—no matter how small
- Celebrate your giving moments

Chapter 11: Practical Tools for Your Journey

You've come so far.

You've envisioned your legacy, built a blueprint, and started laying the foundations for your children's future.

Now, it's time to put your plans into motion.

This chapter is your action hub—filled with the practical tools, templates, checklists, planners, and trackers that help turn ideas into routines, and routines into results.

Whether you're just getting started or fine-tuning what already works, this toolkit is designed to meet you exactly where you are.

Because you don't need to be perfect.

You just need a plan that honors your purpose.

Job Description Templates

Assign real, meaningful roles to your children based on their age, skills, and your business needs.

Example: Content Assistant (Ages 12–15)

- Tasks: Write YouTube descriptions, schedule posts in Canva, brainstorm titles
- Skills Required: Basic writing, organization
- Pay Range: $8–$10/hour
- Learning Outcome: SEO, scheduling tools, content strategy

Example: Inventory Manager (Ages 10–12)

- Tasks: Count vending stock, organize supplies, report shortages
- Pay Range: $6–$8/hour
- Learning Outcome: Organization, tracking systems, responsibility

Tip: Print and keep copies of signed agreements in a family business binder.

Timesheet Log

Track hours worked to stay IRS-compliant and model healthy financial habits.

Date	Child's Name	Job Title	Task Completed	Hours	Rate	Total Pay
7/15	Elijah	Inventory	Stocked machines	2	$7	$14

- Store logs digitally or in a physical payroll folder
- Include signatures if possible
- File monthly with your bookkeeping records

Financial Setup Checklist

Create a child-friendly financial system:

- Open youth checking/savings account
- Set up Roth IRA (for earned income)
- Open custodial investment account (UTMA/UGMA)
- Order debit card (Greenlight, Capital One MONEY)
- Create a simple budget worksheet
- Link accounts to a parent-monitored app

Pro Tip: Involve your child in the setup—explain why each tool matters.

Family Vision Planner

Define your legacy with intention.

Family Values:

Choose 3–5 (e.g., faith, ownership, service, creativity, honesty)

Mission Statement Example:

"We are a family that creates with love, serves with purpose, and builds wealth together."

Short-Term Goals (Next 90 Days):

1. Hire kids legally and track hours
2. Launch family YouTube series
3. Open investment account for each child

Long-Term Goals (1–5 Years):

- Buy family land
- Publish 3 books
- Pass down business systems to teens
- Create a family giving foundation

Monthly Review Tracker

Use this for regular check-ins to keep momentum:

Month	Business Income	Savings Added	Investment Grown	Giving Completed	Lessons Learned
July	$3,200	$300	+$150	Donated $25 to backpack drive	Kids learned to use Canva!

- Make it a family ritual
- Celebrate wins and lessons
- Adjust goals monthly

Emergency Info & Succession Snapshot

Begin your ownership and emergency planning here:

- Business Overview (name, EIN, income streams)
- Important Logins (banking, YouTube, Shopify)
- Key Contacts (attorney, CPA, coach)
- Successor(s) and their roles
- Will and estate plan status
- Insurance policies
- Document storage locations

📌 Tip: Create a Legacy Binder or secure digital folder with this info.

Bonus: Family Finance Glossary

Stick this in your homeschool binder or on the fridge!

Term	Kid-Friendly Definition
Budget	A plan for your money—how you'll use it wisely
Savings	Money you put away for later
Investment	Money that grows over time
Credit Score	A grade for how well you repay borrowed money
Asset	Something that adds money to your pocket
Liability	Something that costs you money
Legacy	What you leave behind for others
Passive Income	Money you earn while you sleep

- Add a new word each month
- Use during games or dinner conversations

⚖ Reflection | Prayer | Affirmation | Action

Practical Tools for Your Journey

Reflection Questions

1. Which tool are you most excited to try?
2. What small step can you take this week to get organized?
3. How can you include your children in using these tools?
4. What system could you start documenting today?

Affirmation

"My systems are sacred. I am building structure that supports peace, legacy, and generational freedom."

Prayer

Dear Lord,

Thank You for giving me the tools I need to walk in wisdom and prepare for the future.

Help me to use these systems not as burdens, but as blessings.

Guide my hands as I build structure for my children's success.

Let our household reflect order, stewardship, and joy. May every form, folder, and financial step bring us closer to purpose, peace, and legacy. Amen.

Action

Choose 3 to complete this week:

- Fill out one job description per child
- Print and start using the timesheet log
- Set up or review your child's savings or IRA
- Write your family mission statement
- Post your finance glossary somewhere visible
- Schedule your first Monthly Review Day

Chapter 12: Keep Building, Keep Believing

You've reached the final pages of this guide—but this is not the end of your story.

It's the beginning of a new, purposeful chapter you are writing for your family.

By picking up this book and choosing to plan ahead, you've already shown something powerful:

- You are not just surviving.
- You are not just hustling for today.
- You are building something that will outlast you.

This is what legacy looks like:

1. Teaching your child to save their first $20
2. Paying them fairly for their time and creativity
3. Documenting systems to protect their future
4. Daring to believe that you—yes, you—can create generational wealth

Legacy Is Not About Perfection

You don't have to get it all right.

You don't need a flawless business or a perfect credit score.

What matters is that you keep showing up:

- For your children
- For your vision
- For the little girl you once were—the one who dreamed of more even when life was hard

This Is Just the Beginning

Every lesson you teach your children ripples forward.

Every hour you spend building systems, income, and structure plants seeds that will bear fruit—maybe even in generations you'll never meet.

That's the beauty of legacy:

It's measured not just in money, but in doors opened, wisdom passed on, and love put into action.

When It Feels Hard, Remember:

1. You are not alone.
2. You are not behind.
3. You are not unqualified.

You are a Warrior Mom.

You are an architect of freedom.

You are living proof that pain can be turned into purpose—and purpose into prosperity.

Keep Building

- Build systems that serve your family while you rest
- Build your children's confidence and financial literacy
- Build the belief that your story matters

Keep Believing

- Believe that small steps create big change
- Believe your sacrifices are seen—and multiplied
- Believe wealth is about love in motion

🐦 Reflection | Prayer | Affirmation | Action

Keep Building, Keep Believing

Final Reflection

As you close this book, pause to breathe in this truth:

You are enough.

You are capable.

You are already leaving a legacy.

Affirmation

"I am the legacy. I am the foundation. I am the light guiding my family toward freedom, purpose, and peace."

Prayer

God, Thank You for walking with me through every page of this journey.

I release the fear of not being enough and embrace the truth that You've equipped me for this.

Strengthen me to keep building. Renew my faith when I feel weary.

Let my children see You through my actions, my vision, and my love.

May everything I do point toward Your goodness and the legacy You've called me to leave. Amen.

Action Your Next Steps

- Revisit a chapter and implement something new
- Set your first Family Review Day
- Keep this guide close—use it often
- Share what you've learned with another parent
- Celebrate how far you've come—you are changing your family's story

Final Note from the Author

Dear Warrior Mom,

You made it to the end—and I hope you know how powerful that is.

This wasn't just a book. It was a baton being passed—from my heart to your hands, from one tired-but-determined mama to another, from one legacy builder to the next.

You didn't need permission to rise—but if you ever doubted you could, I hope this guide was your reminder:

You can. You were made for this. You are already doing it.

Don't wait to be perfect. Don't wait to be rich. Don't wait until the pain is gone. Build anyway. Teach anyway. Lead anyway. Love anyway.

Even on your hardest days, remember: your presence, your plans, and your prayers are planting seeds that will grow long after you're gone.

Keep dreaming. Keep teaching. Keep building. Keep believing. The world needs the legacy only you can create.

With grit, grace, and generational vision, Shaun

Scriptures for Wisdom & Abundance

Proverbs 13:22 (NLT)

A good person leaves an inheritance for their children's children.

Deuteronomy 8:18 (NLT)

It is God who gives you the ability to produce wealth.

Luke 16:10 (NLT)

Whoever is faithful with very little is also faithful with much.

James 1:5 (NLT)

If you need wisdom, ask God, and He will gladly give it to you.

Closing Prayer:

Lord, guide my decisions, help me steward well, and let my family prosper in wisdom, faith, and abundance.

Book Club & Reflection Questions

Use these questions for small groups, accountability partners, church study groups, or personal journaling:

1. What was your biggest "aha moment" while reading this guide?
2. Which legacy planning step feels most urgent for your family right now?
3. How do you currently model financial habits for your children? What would you like to change or strengthen?
4. What limiting beliefs about money or legacy did you identify during this journey?
5. How can you involve your children more in your business, planning, or wealth conversations?
6. What does "legacy" mean to you personally—and how has that meaning shifted after reading this book?
7. What chapter would you recommend another mom read first—and why?
8. Who in your life do you want to pass this book to?
9. What fears came up during this process—and how did you push through?
10. How will you celebrate yourself for taking these steps?

Glossary of Key Terms

A quick-reference guide for Warrior Moms building family wealth and legacy.

I've created this comprehensive glossary of terms for a mom just learning about these topics. I kept the definitions clear, approachable, and practical, avoiding overly technical jargon. Use it as a steppingstone to building your wealth vocabulary.

A

Assets – Anything your family owns with value, like cash, property, or investments.

Allowance – Money given regularly to children for spending, saving, or giving.

B

Budget – A plan for earning, saving, spending, and giving money.

Beneficiary – A person who receives money or property from a will, trust, or insurance policy.

Business Expenses – Costs for running your business, such as supplies or marketing.

Business Income – Money your business earns before expenses.

C

Cash Flow – Money moving in and out of your family or business. Positive means you earn more than you spend.

Children's Jobs (Family Business) – Real, age-appropriate tasks your kids can do in your business to earn money legally.

Credit Score – A number showing how responsible someone is with borrowing and paying back money.

D

Debt – Money owed to someone else, like a loan or credit card balance.

Diversification – Spreading investments across different assets to reduce risk.

Dependent – A child or family member you financially support.

E

Earnings – Money received from work, business, or investments.

Education Savings Account (ESA/529) – Accounts to save for a child's future education with tax advantages.

Estate Planning – Preparing legal documents to manage your assets when you pass away.

F

Family Business Blueprint – A structured plan for running a business with family members.

Financial Literacy – Understanding how money works: earning, saving, spending, giving, and investing.

Financial Goal – A target for your money, like saving for a home or an emergency fund.

Financial Independence – Having enough income and savings to live without relying on others.

G

Giving / Charitable Giving – Using money or time to help others and teach purpose to your children.

Gross Income – Total money earned before taxes or deductions.

H

Hiring Your Children Legally – Following IRS rules so your kids can earn money in your business without causing tax issues.

Hourly Wage / Salary – Hourly is paid per hour; salary is a fixed amount over time.

I

Income Tax – Money paid to the government on what you earn.

Inheritance – Assets or money received from someone who has passed away.

Investments – Money put into something (stocks, bonds, business) to grow over time.

L

Legacy – The lasting impact, values, and wealth you leave for your children or family.

Liabilities – Money your family or business owes, like loans or bills.

Living Trust – Legal document that holds assets for heirs and avoids probate court.

O

Ownership / Equity – Legal rights to something, like part of a business or property.

Opportunity Cost – What you give up when choosing one financial decision over another.

P

Payroll – The system of paying employees, including children, correctly and legally.

Power of Attorney – Legal permission for someone to make decisions for you if you can't.

Profit – Money left after expenses are paid.

Purposeful Payment – Paying children in a way that teaches money lessons.

R

Roth IRA – A retirement account where money grows tax-free; children with earned income can have one.

Revenue – Total income from business or work before expenses.

S

Savings Account – A bank account used to store money and earn interest.

Self-Employment Tax – Tax paid by business owners on their earnings.

Succession Plan – Plan for transferring business ownership or leadership to the next generation.

Stock / Shares – Owning a small part of a company.

Spending Plan – How money will be used over time, part of a budget.

T

Taxes – Money paid to the government on income, property, or sales.

Trust Fund – Fund managed by someone for the benefit of another, often a child.

Tax Deduction – Money subtracted from taxable income.

V

Value Proposition – Explains why someone should buy your product or service.

W

Wealth – Includes money, assets, skills, knowledge, and opportunities passed to the next generation.

Will – Legal document stating how your assets are distributed after death.

Work Ethic – Habits and values around completing tasks, showing responsibility, and being reliable.

Resources & Recommended Tools

Financial Tools for Families:

- Greenlight Debit Card for Kids – Teach budgeting, saving, and giving with parental oversight
- Fidelity Youth Roth IRA – Set up a retirement account for teens with earned income
- Capital One MONEY Teen Account – Free, easy-to-use banking for families

Content & Course Tools:

- Stan Store – Sell books, digital products, coaching sessions, or affiliate links
- Teachable – Build and sell online courses or workshops
- Canva – Design planners, checklists, business flyers, and digital curriculum

Business & Payroll Setup:

- Gusto or QuickBooks Payroll – Legally pay your children and stay IRS-compliant
- IRS Publication 15 – Employer's Tax Guide

- IRS Family Employment Rules – Understand your rights and responsibilities as a parent-employer

Educational Books for Kids:

- Finance 101 for Kids by Walter Andal
- I Am A Leader: A 90-Day Leadership Journal for Kids by Peter J. Liang
- The Richest Man in Babylon: Teen Edition by George S. Clason

The Warrior Mom's Guide™ Book Series

FOUNDATION: The Pilot Book

♡ A Warrior Within, A Chronic Illness

The Warrior Mom's Guide to Sickle Cell & Chronic Resilience

My story of battling sickle cell while raising a family—woven with practical mindset shifts, survival tools, and advocacy.

📖 The heart of the Warrior Mom movement and the introduction to the series.

THE DEEP-DIVE SERIES (Books 1–10)

🩶 **The Warrior Mom's Guide to GhettoOCD™** (Home Organization & Cleaning)

Practical, real-life homemaking strategies for moms with chronic illness.

🌸 **The Warrior Mom's Guide to Mental Wellness & Finding Joy in the Chaos**

Therapy, prayer, and emotional survival tools for weary moms.

🩶 The Warrior Mom's Guide to Single Motherhood by Choice

Reclaiming peace, health, and wholeness after carrying it all.

🩶 The Warrior Mom's Guide to Loving Unexpectedly

Guardianship, Fostering & Adoption with Faith and Fierce Love

Finding your voice, courage, and confidence in nontraditional motherhood.

🩶 The Warrior Mom's Guide to Generational Wealth & Family Legacy

Building wealth, purpose, and a future that lasts.

🩶 The Warrior Mom's Guide to Spiritual Reset & Chronic Faith

Faith after diagnosis, grace during flare-ups, and spiritual renewal when you feel forgotten.

The Warrior Mom's Guide to ZBB & Cash Stuffing (Finances)

Zero-based budgeting & cash envelope systems for sick-day survival.

The Warrior Mom's Guide to Homeschooling for the Homegirls

Practical tools for rest, rejuvenation, and chronic-illness-friendly homeschooling.

The Warrior Mom's Guide to Homeownership & Stability

Creative paths to securing a home with chronic illness and limited income.

The Warrior Mom's Guide to Living in Peace

End-of-life planning with grace: wills, medical directives, legacy projects, and restoration.

Find the books, companion workbooks, journals, planners, and more at:

www.warriormomacademy.com

About the Author

Shaun M. G. Harris is a writer, speaker, entrepreneur, and unapologetic Warrior Mom.

As a single mother of four and a chronic illness survivor living with sickle cell disease, she empowers mothers—especially those navigating health, hardship, and hustle.

Shaun is the creator of The Warrior Mom's Guide series, offering guidance on homeownership, homeschooling, estate planning, spiritual healing, and financial legacy.

Her writing blends real-life wisdom, faith, and practical tools to help mothers build lives they don't need a break from.

Through books, courses, coaching, and her upcoming podcast The Warrior Mom Book Talk, Shaun equips mamas to walk in power, prepare with peace, and parent with purpose.

Acknowledgments

I'd like to thank God—thank You for turning my pain into purpose.

To every mother reading this:

You are the heartbeat of your home, the backbone of your family, and the legacy builder they will never forget.

Thank you for daring to dream beyond survival. Thank you for saying yes to the hard work of healing, planning, and preparing.

To my children—my why, my legacy, my miracles— you are the reason I keep going.

To every friend, sister, reader, and soul who ever believed in me, edited a page, or prayed me through a flare: I carry you with me. This book is for us.

THE WARRIOR MOM GUIDES

www.ingramcontent.com/pod-product-compliance
Lightning Source LLC
Chambersburg PA
CBHW021940190326
41519CB00009B/1081